PRIVATE EYE'S

Colemanballs
4

A selection of quotes, most
of which originally appeared in
PRIVATE EYE's 'Colemanballs'
column.
Once again, our thanks
to the readers who
sent us their
contributions.

If you enjoyed this book,
the best-selling first

Colemanballs

is still available, as are

Colemanballs 2 and 3

COLEMANBALL'S TOP TEN

Place	Name	Entries
1	David Coleman	59
2	Murray Walker	43
3	Simon Bates	28
	Ted Lowe	28
4	Ron Pickering	25
5	Peter Jones	20
6	Harry Carpenter	19
7	Brian Moore	17
8	Bryon Butler	15
9	Trevor Bailey	14
10	Peter Powell	13

Figures compiled by the Neasden Institute of Statistics. E&OE

PRIVATE EYE's
Colemanballs
4

Compiled and edited by
Barry Fantoni

Illustrated by Larry

PRIVATE EYE/ANDRÉ DEUTSCH

Published in Great Britain 1988 by
Private Eye Productions Limited,
6 Carlisle Street, London W1

In association with André Deutsch Limited
105-106 Great Russell Street, London WC1

9 8 7 6 5 4 3 2 1

ISBN 0 233 98337 6

Typeset by JH Graphics Ltd, Reading

Printed in Great Britain by
Richard Clay (The Chaucer Press) Ltd
Bungay, Suffolk

Athletics

Zola Budd: so small, so waif-like, you literally
can't see her. But there she is.

ALAN PARRY

It's the first indoor outing this year.

ALAN PARRY

There's going to be a real ding-dong when the bell goes.

DAVID COLEMAN

This could be a repeat of what will happen at the European Games next week.

DAVID COLEMAN

Not only is Sebastian Coe looking cool, calm and collected, he's hardly breathing.

RON PICKERING

One of the great unknown champions because very little is known about him.

DAVID COLEMAN

Valerie Briscoe-Hooks runs on a knife-edge of commitment in this race.

RON PICKERING

McKeen will sit on Cram's shoulder and hope to be lifted by the crowd.

COMMENTATOR

You were treading where no man fears to go . . .

RON PICKERING

Ernest Vettori, the man of the moment, last year.

RON PICKERING

Obviously on paper it's a very good game. Do you think, in theory, it'll be one?

ANDREW GIDDLEY

All three girls, medallists in the Commonwealth Games, continue their duel.

PETER MATTHEWS

When the pace is slow like this, sometimes the athletes will make a move they hadn't planned to make earlier in the race than they planned to do it.

BRENDAN FOSTER

Charlie (Spedding), who believes in an even pace and hopes to run the second part of the race faster than the first.

DAVID COLEMAN

We nurture our losers better than any country in the world.

RON PICKERING

She's held the Americans all the way to the line if not all the way to the line.

RON PICKERING

You have to talk in metres because nobody under 16 understands feet nowadays. The course is 1.6 miles long . . .

DAVID VINE

Panetta was silver medallist in the European championships, when he led all the way

DAVID COLEMAN

She's not Ben Johnson, but then who is?

DAVID COLEMAN

The Italians are hoping for an Italian victory.

DAVID COLEMAN

The reason she's so fast over the hurdles is because she's so fast between them.

DAVID COLEMAN

This race is all about racing.

DAVID COLEMAN

Watch the time — it gives you a good indication of
how fast they're running.

RON PICKERING

The news from the javelin is that it was won by
that winning throw we saw earlier.

DAVID COLEMAN

Of course it doesn't mean anything, but what it
does mean is that Bile is very relaxed.

DAVID COLEMAN

No problems for Zubriggen. He just sits, stands
and waits.

DAVID VINE

That would have won him the gold medal in the Championship four years ago which he won anyway.

DESMOND LYNAM

He's got to stick the boot in, to use a technical term.

STEVE OVETT

Henry Marsh, the tail-ender, is right at the back.

RON PICKERING

If this boy keeps his head and keeps running, the sky's at his feet.

GEORGE BLACKBURN

One thing I must say about this packed meeting, it is absolutely packed.

RON PICKERING

Dave Bedford, the athlete of all time in the 1970s.

DAVID COLEMAN

And there go the two leaders — Boutayeb, Aouita and Baccouche.

DAVID COLEMAN

Ben Johnson! He's like Concorde! Off the blocks like a caged tiger!

STUART HALL

At the moment Petranoff is ahead by virtue of his position at the moment.

RON PICKERING

And the crowd absolutely standing in their seats.

RON PICKERING

American Football

There are no opportune times for a penalty, and this is not one of those times.

JACK YOUNGBLOOD

And Harrera is now climbing like a metronome.

PAUL SHERWEN

Boxing

My mum says I used to fight my way out of the cot. But I can't remember. That was before my time.

FRANK BRUNO

Bruno's strength, in fact, is his strength.

REG GUTTERIDGE

DAVID FROST: 'So who's been your greatest inspiration, outside boxing?'
FRANK BRUNO: 'Er . . . I think Joe Louis.'

Round 1. Start of the fight, in fact.

DESMOND LYNAM

He certainly handed out more than he gave.

HARRY CARPENTER

That's cricket, Harry, you get these sort of things in boxing.

FRANK BRUNO

At the finish, it was all over.

JIM WATT

INTERVIEWER: 'It's beginning to look like a reality, Frank.'
FRANK BRUNO: 'Yeah, it's a reality which looks like coming true!'

I would like to retire with my brains still in contact.

ERROL GRAHAM

His face was a mask of blood, I think he must have a cut somewhere.

HENRY COOPER

I've never seen a Mexican pushover boxer and this man certainly isn't one of them.

HARRY CARPENTER

Frank Bruno will definitely fight Mike Tyson — that's a fact of life.

MICKEY DUFF

Cricket

In Hampshire's innings the Smith brothers scored 13 and 52 respectively.

HENRY BLOFIELD

I don't think cricket should be used as a political football.

DAVID GRAVENEY

That's what happens when, in cricketing parlance,
the wheel comes off — and you can't steer the boat.
BOB WILLIS

England were beaten in the sense that they lost.
DICKIE DAVIS

He has got perfect control over the ball right up to
the minute he lets it go.
PETER WALKER

The only possible result is a draw. The alternative is a win for England.

RICHIE BENAUD

Yes, he's a very good cricketer — pity he's not a better batter or bowler.

TOM GRAVENEY

Mudassar has really put the icing on the day for the visitors.

JACK BANNISTER

The wicket didn't do too much, but when it did, it did too much.

MIKE GATTING

Gary never had a nickname — he was always called either Gary or The King.

PAT POCOCK

Kapil Dav joins Ian Botham in the record books as the only cricketer to reach the double of 3,000 test runs and 300 test wickets.

RICHARD KEYS

And as so often with the Achilles tendon injuries, the Achilles goes.

PAT POCOCK

This is really a fairy book start.

BOB WILLIS

Vengsarkar taking a simple catch at square leg, the
ball literally dropping down his throat.

BOB WILLIS

Cycling

He's speeding away like a jack in the box.

PAUL GERSHWIN

The field is not very far behind and these two are
not very far in front.

LWT COMMENTATOR

Darts

There's only one way to go from this, sixty double ten or twenty twenty double top.

ERIC BRISTOW

But, for Anderson that step has become a chasm.

TONY GUBBA

Football

Never go for a 50/50 ball unless you are 80/20 sure . . .

IAN DARK

Referee Norlinger is outstanding in the sense that he stands out!

GEORGE HAMILTON

And there's Ray Clemence looking as cool as ever
out in the cold.

JIMMY HILL

You've got to believe that you're going to win and I
believe that we'll win the world cup until the final
whistle blows and we're knocked out.

PETER SHILTON

IAN ST JOHN: 'It's a real battle tomorrow with
Brazil against Spain. What do you reckon, Bruce?'
BRUCE GROBBELAR: 'Well, I've got to go for
the Italians on this one, Saint.'

. . . and the news from Guadalajara, where the temperature is a staggering 96 degrees, is that Falcao is warming up.

BRIAN MOORE

Shilton looks at the ground: 'Is this a spot I see before me?'

BARRY DAVIES

If history is going to repeat itself I should think we can expect the same thing again.

TERRY VENABLES

Brazil, the favourites — if they are the favourites, which they are.

BRIAN CLOUGH

I'm not a believer in luck . . . but I do believe you need it.

ALAN BALL

The Uruguayans are losing no time in making a meal around the referee.

MIKE INGHAM

The Danes are probing for position — everyone of them somewhere on the pitch.

ITV

The World Cup — truly an international event.

JOHN MOTSON

This is the first time Denmark has ever reached the World Cup Finals, so this is the most significant moment in Danish history.

JOHN HELM

Such a positive move by Uruguay, bringing two players off and putting two players on.

JOHN HELM

I think that was a moment of cool panic there.

RON ATKINSON

Beckenbauer really has gambled all his eggs.

RON ATKINSON

West Germany's Breigel hasn't been able to get past anyone yet — that's his trademark.

JOHN HELM

Nearly all the Brazilian supporters are wearing yellow shirts. It's a fabulous kaleidoscope of colour.

JOHN MOTSON

I don't think that there's anyone bigger or smaller than Maradona.

KEVIN KEEGAN

Celtic manager Davie Hay still has a fresh pair of legs up his sleeve.

JOHN GREIG

If a week is a long time in politics then for Ron Atkinson's Manchester United the last seven days have been an equinox.

STUART HALL

I spent four indifferent years at Goodison, but they were great years.

MARTIN HODGE

Souness gave Fleck a second chance and he grabbed it with both feet.

JAMES SANDERSON

That's Robson — a totally convicted player.
JIMMY ARMFIELD

They've missed so many chances they must be
wringing their heads in shame.
RON GREENWOOD

They're floating up on a sea of euphoria, and
hoping to drag themselves clear of the quicksand at
the bottom . . .
PETER JONES

It's headed away by John Clark, using his head.
DEREK RAE

Tottenham are trying tonight to become the first London team to win this Cup. The last team to do so was the 1973 Spurs team.

MIKE INGHAM

Poor Graham Shaw. It was there for the asking and he didn't give the answer.

PETER JONES

It's the only way we can lose, irrespective of the result.

GRAHAM TAYLOR

It's going to take a shoehorn to prise these two teams apart.

ALAN PARRY

He's very fast and if he gets a yard ahead of himself nobody will catch him.

BOBBY ROBSON

Peter Reid is hobbling, and I've got a feeling that that will slow him down.

JOHN MOTSON

The shot from Laws was precise but wide.

ALAN PARRY

And Southampton have most assuredly lost their confidence in this second half.

MIKE McGEE

. . . where at Southampton they conceded a two goal lead . . .

CLIVE TYLDESLEY

Dewalt had all kinds of time momentarily.

PAT MARSDEN

The game is balanced in Arsenal's favour.

JOHN MOTSON

Merseyside derbies usually last 90 minutes and I'm sure today's won't be any different.

TREVOR BROOKING

And the bald head of John Sillett leaps from the Coventry bench.

STUART LINNELL

Many clubs have a question mark in the shape of an axehead hanging over them.

MALCOLM MACDONALD

If we get promotion, let's sit down and see where we stand.

ROY McFARLAND

. . . as Whiteside philosophically makes his way to the far post.

MARTIN TYLER

Their football was exceptionally good . . . and they played some good football.

BOBBY ROBSON

Arsenal's team-work is their strength — along with getting men between the ball.

MIKE BURTON

Tottenham have impressed me. They haven't thrown in the towel even though they've been under the gun.

BOBBY CHARLTON

You've got to miss them to score sometimes.

DAVE BASSETT

That's an old Ipswich move – O'Callaghan crossing for Mariner to drive over the bar.

JOHN MOTSON

Dumbarton player Steve McCahill has limped off with a badly cut forehead.

TOM FERRIE

A contract on a piece of paper, saying you want to leave, is like a piece of paper saying you want to leave.

JOHN HOLLINS

We didn't think we'd come here tonight and get any sort of result.

LES SEALEY

And I honestly believe that we can go all the way to Wembley . . . unless somebody knocks us out.

DAVE BASSETT

It was that game that put the Everton ship back on the road.

ALAN GREEN

And Arsenal now have plenty of time to dictate these last few seconds.

PETER JONES

Bobby Robson must be thinking of throwing some fresh legs on!

KEVIN KEEGAN

Winning isn't the end of the world.

DAVID PLEAT

Rangers are really exerting the screw now . . .
ARCHIE McPHERSON

Unlike the two teams, the Duchess of Kent is here for the second year running.

JOHN MOTSON

What makes this game so delightful is that when both teams get the ball they are attacking their opponents' goal.

JIMMY HILL

Celtic were at one time nine points ahead, but somewhere along the road, their ship went off the rails.

RICHARD PARK

. . . like a predator about to devour the target.

ALAN PARRY

Jim McLean, one of the few managers who can physically lift a side.

ARTHUR MONTFORD

That's football, Mike, Northern Ireland have had several chances and haven't scored but England had no chances and scored twice.

TREVOR BROOKING

. . . and so they have not been able to improve their 100 per cent record.

SPORTS ROUNDUP

In terms of the Richter Scale this defeat was a force eight gale.

JOHN LYALL

Outside of quality we had other qualities.

BERTIE MEE

In comparison, there's no comparison.

RON GREENWOOD

I would also think that the action replay showed it to be worse than it actually was, Brian.

RON ATKINSON

Mirandinha will have more shots this afternoon
than both sides put together.

MALCOLM MACDONALD

Newcastle, of course, unbeaten in their last five
wins.

BRIAN MOORE

Football's not like an electric light. You can't just
flick the button and change from slow to quick.

JOHN GREIG

Certain people are for me, certain people are
pro me.

TERRY VENABLES

I'm going to make a prediction − it could go either
way.

RON ATKINSON

And with just 4 minutes gone, the score is
already 0−0.

IAN DARK

They've got their feet on the ground and if they
stay that way they'll go places.

JOHN GIDMAN

I was disappointed to leave Spurs, but quite pleased
that I did.

STEVE PERRYMAN

Being naturally right-footed he doesn't often chance
his arm with his left foot.

TREVOR BROOKING

. . . and history seems to be going out of the window for Walsall.

ANDY GRAY

It's understandable and I understand that.

TERRY VENABLES

. . . and Radcliffe, as befits his name, rattled Starbuck from behind . . .

JOHN MOTSON

The Arsenal defence is skating close to the wind.
JACKIE CHARLTON

We know what we need to do now so I think we'll
either win or lose.

IAN RUSH

And sitting on the Watford bench is Ernie
Whalley's brother Tom. Both Welshmen.
BRIAN MOORE

You get some Scots coming down to London to manage but by the same alternative, you don't get Englishmen going up there to manage.

DAVE BASSETT

Strangely, in slow motion replay, the ball seemed to hang in the air for even longer.

DAVID ACFIELD

He (Platini) was given a great reception when he went off.

ELTON WELSBY

Hoddle hasn't been the Hoddle we know. Neither has Robson.

RON GREENWOOD

They've flown in from all over the world, have the rest of the world team.

BRIAN MOORE

He has a great understanding of where the goalkeeper is in relation to the goal.

DAVID PLEAT

Ian Baird is dashing around like a steamroller up front.

MARTIN TYLER

He'll be giving everything, but he hasn't got everything to give.

IAN ST JOHN

And Rush, quick as a needle.

RON JONES

BRYON BUTLER: 'Did you have any doubts
about yourself when you left Tottenham?'
PETER SHREEVE: 'I don't think so.'

Fine tackling by Butcher using his telescopic legs.
                                    JOCK BROWN

Golf

But can Watson stop the tide that Mark McNulty is running on?

LOUIS KARPAS

Azinger is wearing an all black outfit: black jumper, blue trousers, white shoes and a pink 'tea cosy' hat.

RENTON LAIDLAW

He's the youngest player on both sides.

PETER ALLISS

Horses

The next race has been literally decimated — half the ten runners have been withdrawn.

JULIAN WILSON

These American horses know the fences like the back of their hands.

HARVEY SMITH

It's a photo between Gold Prospect and Shareblank and third is probably just in behind these two.

PETER O'SULLEVAN

Princess Anne's horse is literally eating up the ground.

PETER BROMLEY

Motorsport

The advantage of the rain is, that if you have a quick bike, there's no advantage.

BARRY SHEENE

In motor racing the ever-present danger is always there.

JOHN WATSON

Senna with the big advantage of being in front.

JAMES HUNT

You can see now that the gap between Mansell and Piquet is rather more than just visual!

MURRAY WALKER

He is shedding buckets of adrenalin in that car.

MURRAY WALKER

Warwick has overtaken Alan Jones and, in the
process, moved up a place . . .

MURRAY WALKER

And Nelson Piquet must be furious with himself
inside his helmet!

MURRAY WALKER

Just under ten seconds for Nigel Mansell — call it
nine point five seconds in round figures.

MURRAY WALKER

I can't imagine what kind of problem Senna has. I
imagine it must be some sort of grip problem.

MURRAY WALKER

The crowd holds its joint breath.

MURRAY WALKER

Whatever is wrong with Arnoux's engine would be
irremediable in the time it takes to do it.

MURRAY WALKER

Alboretto has dropped back up to fifth place.

MURRAY WALKER

As you look at the first four, the significant thing is that Alboretto is fifth.

MURRAY WALKER

And next week we have the Brazilian Grand Prix, which is in Brazil.

BBC WORLD SERVICE

I do think the Europeans have had this attitude that no one could really impregnate their superiority.

JACKIE STEWART

I imagine that the conditions in those cars today are totally unimaginable.

MURRAY WALKER

Anything happens in Grand Prix racing and it usually does.

MURRAY WALKER

Do my eyes deceive me, or is Senna's Lotus sounding a bit rough.

MURRAY WALKER

He's watching us from hospital with his injured
knee.

MURRAY WALKER

It looks like adrenalin is a good disinfectant.

MURRAY WALKER

And as they go round their knees literally kiss the
ground.

MURRAY WALKER

With half the race gone, there is half the race still
to go.

MURRAY WALKER

We're looking at the man who won in '83, '85 and '86, so this could be his hat-trick.

MURRAY WALKER

He's obviously gone in for a wheel change. I say 'obviously' because I can't see it.

MURRAY WALKER

And the Ferrari pits are literally a forest of yellow and black as the mechanics gather together.

MURRAY WALKER

Oddballs

This film is like *King Lear* rewritten by the author of *Henry V*.

ERIC ROTE

So if you haven't set off for the centre yet, the best thing to do is to turn back and go home.

ANNE NIGHTINGALE

. . . and the sands of time ticking away very rapidly.
TOM TYRRELL

He's next door working himself up into a fracas.
SIMON BATES

It's just gone 17 minutes past 4. That's the time, by
the way.

PAUL JORDAN

The worst of it is, is that they don't think any
further than their own noses.
SELINA SCOTT

You must put your foot down with a firm hand.
MICHAEL VAN STRATTEN

Out of those sixty films there were quite a few turkeys. Did you know at the time that some of them were going to stay frogs and not become princes?
BARRY NORMAN

Listen, Jerusalem was not built in a day.
ROBERT MAXWELL

You've really put your finger on the nail there —
that's what it's all about.

BRENDA ELLISON

At the end of the day Stalker goes back to work
tomorrow morning.

DAVID MOFFAT

His brother failed; let's see if he can succeed and
maintain the family tradition.

DAVID COLEMAN

You say you've always had this dream. Tell me,
have you always had this dream?

DAVID FROST

There's a glimpse of a new paper you'll see
tomorrow. It comes out tomorrow.

DAVID FROST

Eye witnesses were on the scene in minutes.

ADAM BOULTON

At the moment we're only scratching at the iceberg.

FARMER

For those of you who haven't read the book, it's
being published tomorrow.

DAVID FROST

There's a lot of good older players around, but very
few.

DAVID CARR

It's been a wet month just about everywhere, but
surprisingly not everywhere.

MICHAEL FISH

Renault are currently enjoying huge losses.
GREG STRANGE

And don't forget — on Sunday you can hear the
two minute silence on Radio One.
STEVE WRIGHT

We are now living in the age in which we live.
ANN BURDIS

Richard Burton had a tremendous passion for the English language, especially the spoken and written word.

FRANK BOUGH

Did you write the words, or the lyrics?

BRUCE FORSYTH

Most of the living legends I've been researching go back over centuries.

ANDREW JONES

It says here, and it is underlined in capital letters.

DEREK JAMESON

It's a one-to-one dialogue. You open your mouth and you're talking to six million people.

DEREK JAMESON

It was here that V.S. Naipaul found his voice as a writer.

MELVYN BRAGG

Almost on all green plant except for the flowers.
ROY LANCASTER

I must declare an interest in this, and say that I
know nothing at all about guns.
JIMMY YOUNG

And we journalists are taught to avoid clichés like
the plague.
IAIN WILSON

It's a can of worms full of Pandora's boxes.
ALAN WATKINS

It was completely quiet in the stadium − but noisy.
JOHN HUMPHREYS

I was driving through Kent and literally went
through bright blue sunshine.

MIKE SMITH

You are a first generation American but your father
wasn't.

ALAN YENTOB

My shoes are size 2½ — the same size as my feet.

ELAINE PAGE

Miss World is still popular even though it has its fair
share of knockers.

JULIA MORLEY

If we can just get young people to do as their fathers
did, that is wear condoms.

RICHARD BRANSON

For many people, homelessness means simply not
having a home.

REVD. DONALD REEVES

Did you ever give a thought to the teams you never think about?

DAVE HODGE

Volunteers are being given fake placebos.

DEREK JAMESON

I've always been a bit more maturer than what I am.

SAMANTHA FOX

. . . through remote Chinese villages where the hand of westerners has never set foot.

JUDY SPEARS

Here's a story that's in two parts in every sense of the word.

SIMON BATES

And he nipped them in the bud, right at the end.

BOB HOLNESS

. . . and let the Government off the hook just when it seemed to be on the run.

HELENA GOODMAN

He gave the world an empire so large the sun couldn't even cast its shadow over it.

DEREK JAMESON

The IBF are digging their heels in at the moment
and they're sticking out like a sore thumb.

IAN BROWN

This kind of thing has happened since
Kingdom Come.

PETER LUSH

I'll tell you one fact — it may be rather boring but
it's interesting.

BARBARA CARTLAND

I think — but this is pure hyperbole on my part —
that may be why people dress like this in
Washington.

SIMON BATES

It's only when you get to the outskirts of the city
that the slippery conditions really get a grip.

NORMAN RICKARD

The champion has retired after eight undefeated
victories.

RICHARD WHITELEY

Direct mail. It falls out of every magazine you open these days.

DEREK JAMESON

Education is as important, if not equally important, for solving the stray dog problem.

DAVID WILKINS, RSPCA

She drowned at the end of her life.

ALAN FRANK

I wonder if we can speak through rose-tinted spectacles?

NICK ROSS

She shrugs her head.

DAVID MERCER

Nigel and I hit it off like a horse on fire.

TONY BRITTON

We have every window-cleaner's dream, self-cleaning windows.

MAGGIE PHILBIN

Penelope Betjeman, who was married to John Betjeman, and was in fact his wife.

RUSSELL HARTY

This could well be the goose that killed the golden egg.

CHESTER COUNCILLOR

The roadworks are set for an indefinite period. We don't know how long that will be.

JOHN HAWKINS

Apparently, there is no truth in the fact that Sylvester Stallone's wife is a lesbian.

STEVE WRIGHT

We would not be here but for those people who gave their lives and very often gave their futures.

SIMON BATES

I've got ten pairs of training shoes, one for every day of the week.

SAMANTHA FOX

.... AND TWENTY BRAS FOR EACH MONTH OF THE YEAR

John Curry is appearing in the play, but he's not wearing his skates - he's got a completely different hat on his head this time.

PETER LEVY

So Carol, you're a housewife and mother. And have you got any children?

MICHAEL BARRYMORE

Not all other people are tarnished with the same brush.

ELTON JOHN

There are only half-a-dozen people with that sort of talent. In my estimation he was a one-off.

DANNY LA RUE

U.S. planes have the capability to penetrate deep into Soviet soil.

GENERAL ROGERS

He's the sort of Admiral I would follow up any hill, anywhere.

LT. COL. OLIVER NORTH

Politics

I have had the most wonderfully loyal and supportive support from the Prime Minister.

SIR MICHAEL HAVERS

A typical example of this government saying one thing with one hand and another thing with the other hand.

ROB GREG

Going back to the motor-car analogy, it's not a matter of buying it off the peg.

DENZIL DAVIES

A week is a long time in politics, and three weeks is twice as long.

ROSIE BARNES

The Health Service is the flower of our nation and it's crumbling.

LABOUR HEALTH SPOKESMAN

We spend weeks and hours every day preparing the budget.

RONALD REAGAN

If you put it on the table as a bargaining chip it becomes a bargaining chip.

RONALD REAGAN

The possibility of an arms agreement between the U.S. and the U.S.S.R. is now a possibility.

PETER HOBDAY

It won't be long before the banana skins start raining down.

PETER KELLNER

They all want to jump on the bandwagon if they see it bearing fruit.

RADIO SCOTLAND

A very gloomy Brian Gould — as always a smile.

DAVID DIMBLEBY

Do you think we are out of the wood yet, or are there more hiccups to come?

BRIAN WIDLAKE

That wasn't the only thing he did. That was just the froth on the cake.

JULIAN CRITCHLEY M.P.

The purpose of this committee is that it can probe where no man fears to go.

BRIAN REDHEAD

Pop

As far as I could see they were laughing at
everybody behind their faces.

SIMON BATES

DAVID 'KID' JENSEN: 'I thought your origins
were strictly in folk music.'
MOIRA BRENNAN: 'Maybe they were but not at
the beginning.'

Steve was the golden halo around the shadow of
failure.

SIMON BATES

Then she met a bloke called Fritz — literally. That
was his name.

SIMON BATES

He's sweating toil and blood out there.

GARY DAVIES

The Rolling Stones suffered a great loss with the death of Ian Stewart, the man who had for so many years played piano quietly and silently with them on stage.

ANDY PEEBLES

It's incredible these days, especially these days!

PETER JAY

My second hit was a flop.

SHAKIN' STEVENS

They literally went to the same school together
from the first day they went there.

SIMON BATES

Sade is currently in Spain, but we've put in a trans-
Atlantic call and here she is.

MIKE SMITH

Not only was Sue having a nervous breakdown, but
she was having a tough time mentally too.

SIMON BATES

And now for some music by George and Ira Gershwin. It's the Ray Noble composition 'But Not For Me'.

EDWARD COLE

Glen Miller who became a legend in his own lifetime due to his early death.

NICHOLAS PARSONS

In our industry John Blake is the kind of guy you either love or hate. I like him.

SIMON BATES

He is in hospital suffering from a nervous breakdown, but no doubt he will soon be better and running around like a maniac.

SIMON BATES

I don't think we're going to get an award tonight . . . I would hedge my bets and say no.

CAROL DECKER (T'PAU)

And going back to last summer, this disc was a big hit, in both senses of the word . . .

MICHAEL MARTIN

It's one of those albums or CDs that you either
have or you don't.

BRUNO BROOKES

Eric Clapton, as everyone knows, is the Clark
Gable of rock music.

SIMON BATES

The concert finishes at 8.00 p.m. so you'll have
plenty of time to get home for the last bus.

SIMON BATES

It was as if a small ten-megaton bomb had gone off.

SIMON BATES

That band are going to be the biggest thing in the world, almost as big as U2.

BRUNO BROOKES

People wonder why I go out with models with nothing between their heads.

SIMON LE BON

The guy's got a great voice — literally.

ANDY PEEBLES

Rowing

Rodney Bewes, a member of the London Rowing Club — that's one of the London clubs.

HARRY CARPENTER

Royal Weddings

And the Abbey is awash with a blaze of colour.
DICKIE ARBITER

And there's the Victoria Memorial, built as a
memorial to Victoria.
DAVID DIMBLEBY

INTERVIEWER: 'Will you be nervous this
afternoon?'
DRESSMAKER: 'Definitely, yes.'
INTERVIEWER: 'About what in particular?'
DRESSMAKER: 'Well there's nothing I can put my
thumb on at the moment.'

L.B.C.

Marble Arch was outside the palace but now
Marble Arch is at Marble Arch.

DAVID DIMBLEBY

. . . a sweet little procession of brides and
bridesmaids . . .

DAVID DIMBLEBY

Rugby

There's no such thing as lack of confidence. You
either have it or you don't.

ROB ANDREW

They've got old shoulders on their heads . . .

J. P. R. WILLIAMS

There's one more Rugby League result to give you,
just to put the jigsaw into focus.

ANDY PEEBLES

Every time he gets the ball he moves around like a
banana-shaped umbrella to cut the park off.

ALEX MURPHY

And they haven't even got a replacement for Hall, even amongst the replacements.

BILL McLAREN

And you really can't take your eyes off this game without seeing something happen!

HARRY GRATION

Every Australian player dreams of playing at Wembley. Because of the atmosphere, and the stigma.

MARK ELIA

Snooker

Yes, after eleven days, we're still sharp as a button here.

DAVID VINE

He won't feel the pressure as much as the more less-experienced players.

DAVID ICKE

Steve Davis — acknowledged by his peers to be the peerless master.

JOHN McCRIRICK

There's no way he can't not go into the final session behind.

DENNIS TAYLOR

He (Dene O'Kane) has really come out bristling on all cylinders.

JACK KARNEHM

The butterflies are certainly flying around Higgins tonight.

TED LOWE

He (John Parrot) has got three frames on the board, but bear in mind he's had to win them to get to that position.

JIM MEADOWCROFT

Well, it's almost impossible to miss, but hitting it is another matter . . .

JIM MEADOWCROFT

As for you, I don't know about me, I'm ready for bed.

DAVID VINE

The laughing Irish eyes are smiling no longer.

TED LOWE

The nerves are fluttering around in his tummy.

TED LOWE

Terry now realises that the only way to win is to play well.

JOHN SPENCER

Of course, one of Stephen Hendry's greatest assets is his ability to score when he's playing.

TED LOWE

If you didn't see Davis against Hendry last night, then you can see it again now.

PRESENTER CHANNEL 4

The frame was one that could go either way but didn't.

BBC2 COMMENTATOR

Well, we're back again tomorrow — all bright and bushy-eyed.

DAVID VINE

They're not only snooker players, they're engineers, taking apart a snooker cue and screwing it back again.

TED LOWE

Tennis

That shot knocked the stuffing out of his sails!
FRU McMILLAN

For the first time a record Wimbledon attendance.
GERALD WILLIAMS

Noah always beats Curren. He has a sort of
Houdini against him.
JOHN LLOYD

There are two Jonas Strensson's on the tour, but
this is the one whose name we'll get more used to
hearing.
GERALD WILLIAMS

Almost perfect symmetry there on the scoreboard:
the 4 and the 3 on the left. If they had been the
same it would have been perfect.
DAN MASKELL

We've had players from all corners of the globe this week — China, Japan, North and South Korea . . .

COMMENTATOR

There is Peter Graf, Steffi's father, with his head on his chin.

DAN MASKELL

Connors is going to have to play without making the sort of errors he didn't make in the third set.

MARK COX

He slips . . . but manages to regroup himself.

DAN MASKELL

Lendl deliberately volleyed the ball straight at his opponent then, something he often does with his passing shots.

JOHN BARRETT

You've got to hand it to Gonzalez, once he saw it
was possible he saw his chance and made it
possible.

DAVID COLEMAN

She puts her head down and bangs it straight across
the line.

ANN JONES